ART OF MODERN ROCK

MINI #2: POSTER GIRLS

BY DENNIS KING

CHRONICLE BOOKS
SAN FRANCISCO

Library of Congress Cataloging-in-Publication Data available.

ISBN: 978-0-8118-6119-9

Manufactured in China.

Book design by Barretto-Co.
Art direction by Dennis King
Cover and spot illustrations by Scrojo

The plate numbers on all pages are ordered from left to right,
top to bottom. Where an additional AoMR plate number appears
at the end of a poster credit, the number refers to its original
plate number in *Art of Modern Rock: The Poster Explosion* by Paul
Grushkin and Dennis King (www.artofmodernrock.com).

10 9 8 7 6 5 4 3 2 1

Chronicle Books LLC
680 Second Street
San Francisco, California 94107

www.chroniclebooks.com

CURVES AHEAD!

IN AN ERA OF POLITICAL CORRECTNESS, THIS BOOK SHOULD PROBABLY INCLUDE IMAGES OF BOTH MEN AND WOMEN AND BE TITLED *POSTER BOYS AND POSTER GIRLS* (BOYS LISTED FIRST ONLY TO CONFORM TO ALPHABETICAL ORDER). SOMEHOW I DON'T THINK THAT THE P.C. CORPS OR ANYONE ELSE WOULD BE INTERESTED IN THAT BOOK.

Emblazoning posters with scantily clad women is a time-honored tradition dating back to Art Nouveau. After all, the purpose of a poster *is* to capture the attention of the viewer. Having observed countless numbers of people stopping to comment on posters in the windows of my gallery, I can safely say that bare breasts are still a showstopper. The evolution of the poster girl from the jackets of back-alley French postcard dealers to the cover of this book is every bit as much about the empowerment of women as it is about the appreciation of the female form, and it's clear that there's something about images of women that resonates with all of us. Whether we choose to attribute that to our earliest bonding with our mothers, to an appreciation of The Divine Feminine, or to prurient interest is a matter of personal inclination. But one thing is certain: if man truly is created in the image of God . . . God must be a woman.

—DENNIS KING, 2008

SKY HIGH HEELS!

Angoramachinegun the smoes @ concert in the park
July 15, 2005 / Cesar Chavez park free

5.1 Mono Men, 1996, Art Chantry
6.1 Angora Machine Gun, 2005, Paul Imagine

8.1 She Wants Revenge, 2006, Adam Turman

DJ BRYAN POLLARD, DJ LIQUID GROOVE AND THERAPY PRESENT:

WEDNESDAY

JAN 15th

DOORS OPEN 7PM

the Flame

21 & UP
WITH PROPER I.D.

3780 PARK BLVD
HILLCREST SAN DIEGO

GET TICKETS FROM ANY
OF DJ BRYAN POLLARD'S
KLUBS & THE FLAME.

An Intimate Encounter With

BJÖRK

OPENING THE SHOW WILL BE THE INFAMOUS DEBBIE DEB!

TICKETS SALES ARE LIMITED!

TICKETS WILL BE $40 IN ADVANCE AND $50 ON THE NIGHT OF SHOW AT THE DOOR.
FOR INFO: WWW.KLUBS.COM-(619) 465-5827   THE FLAME- (619) 295-4163

9.1 Björk, 2003, R. Black

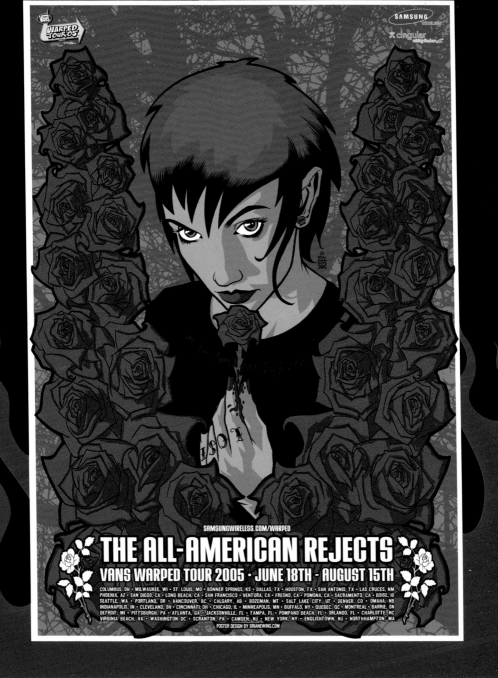

11.1 The All-American Rejects, 2005, Brian Ewing

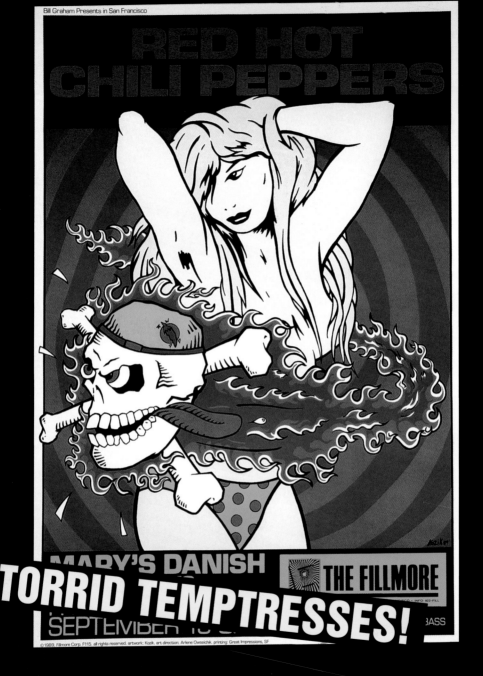

13.1 Brant Bjork and the Bros, 2004, Malleus (AoMR 429.2)

14.1 Man or Astro-Man?, 2000, Marco Almera (AoMR 51.1)

15.1 Death Cab For Cutie, 2004, Scrojo

FEMME FATALES!

16.1 Edith Frost, 2006, Sara Turner (Cricket Press) **16.2** The Never Evers, 2002, Robert Butler (AoMR 417.1)

17.1 Rupa and the April Fishes, 2006, Hugh D'Andrade

19.1 The Decemberists, 2005, Sara Turner (Cricket Press)

VOLUPTUOUS VIXENS!

21.1 N.E.R.D., 2004, Brian Ewing
22.1 B-Side Players, 2002, Scrojo (AoMR 462.2)

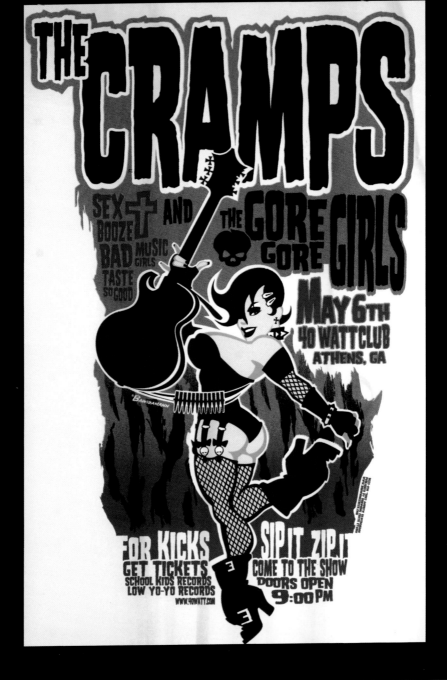

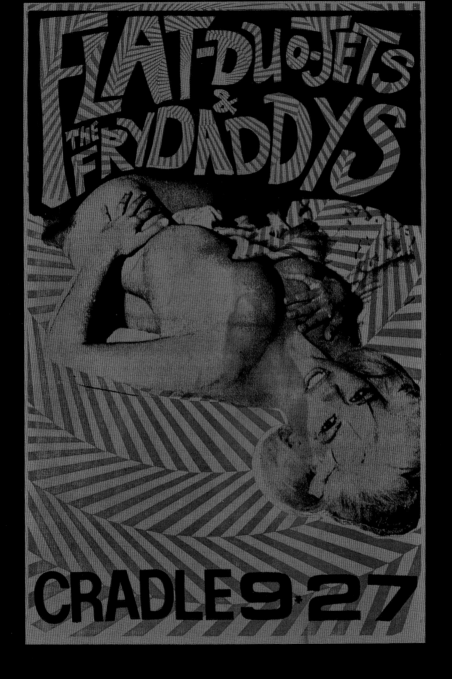

25.1 Flat Duo Jets, 1994, Ron Liberti (AoMR 190.1)

26.1 Perpetual Groove, 2007, Johnny Thief and Jeff Wood (Drowning Creek Studio)

27.1 Song Hospital, 2000, Mister Reusch (AoMR 320.1)

INCENDIARY BLONDES!

Cricket
Press

28.1 "Falling Frogs," 2005, Sara Turner (Cricket Press)

29.1 Concrete Blonde, 2003, Scrojo (AoMR 46707)

DREAMS
FOR SALE

PARTICLE

The
**Flying
Other
Brothers**

A FULL
BIG
GLASS

**THE
GROVE**
1033 NW BOND ST
BEND, OREGON

Friday
1st Sep 2006

© Chris Shaw & The Flying Other Bros.   Artwork: Chris Shaw   Type: Alexandro Fischer   Printing: www.PsPrint.com

www.fob.com

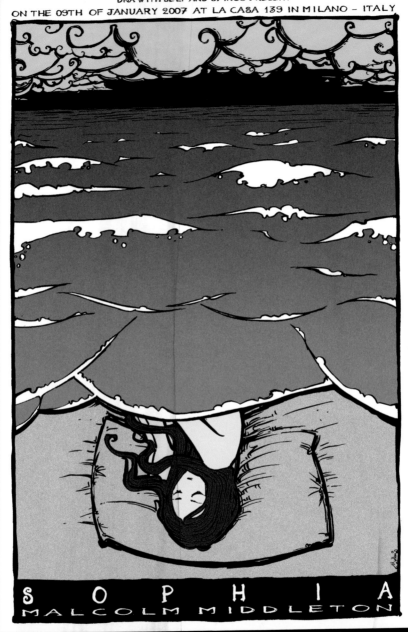

33.1 The Decemberists, 2006, Tara McPherson

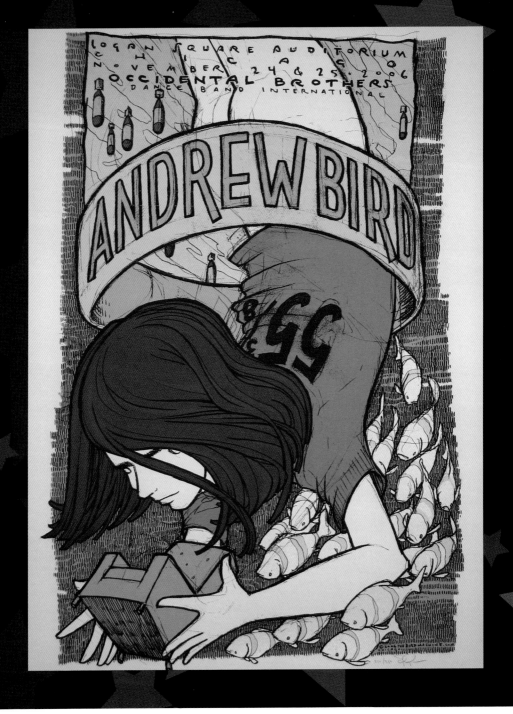

"Nudity can work, but I think it's sexier to

leave more

to the imagination."

– Kristen Thiele

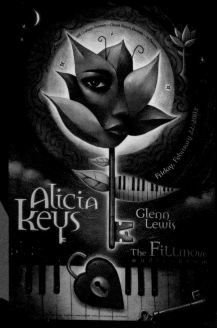

35.1 Qoöl, 2006, Telopa **35.2** Alicia Keys, 2002, Alison Zawacki
(AoMR 334.1) **35.3** Jane's Addiction, 2003, Justin Hampton

36.1 The Psychedelic Furs, 2005, Sara Turner (Cricket Press)

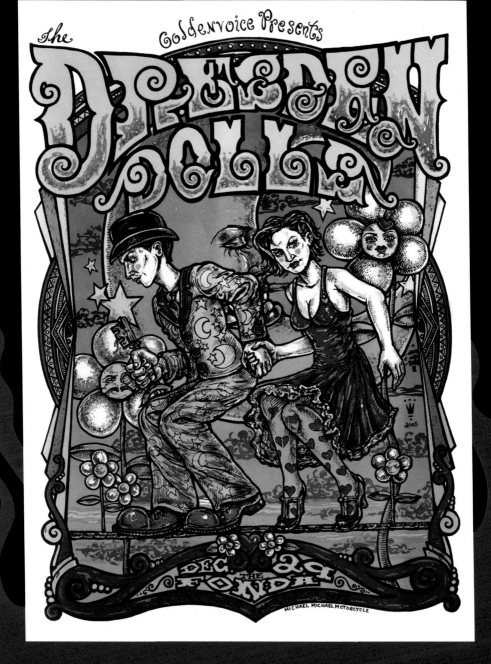

37.1 The Dresden Dolls, 2005, Michael Michael Motorcycle

QUEENS OF THE STONE AGE · 04.14.05 · THROW RAG · THE PREMIERE · SEATTLE

PNE/QOTSA 05-19   WWW.POSTNEOEXPOSIONISM.COM   WWW.JUSTINHAMPTON.COM   WWW.QOTSA.COM

38.1 Queens of the Stone Age, 2005, Justin Hampton

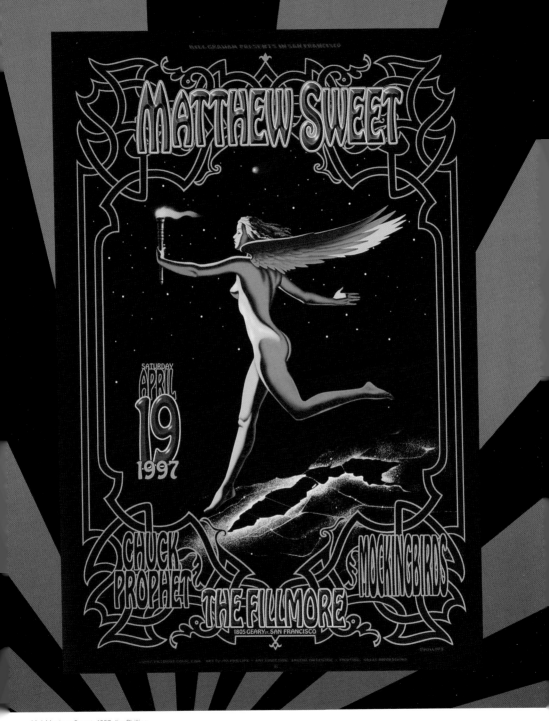

39.1 Matthew Sweet, 1997, Jim Phillips

STRANGE!
FANTASTIC!
TRUE!

© 2002 Dave Gink, www.shadowlandstudios.com

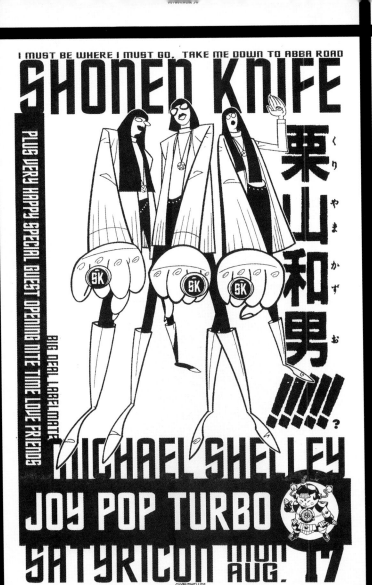

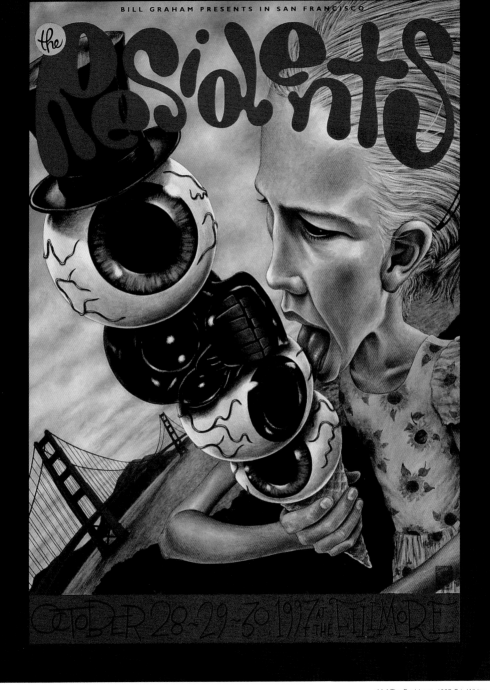

BILL GRAHAM PRESENTS IN SAN FRANCISCO

the Residents

OCTOBER 28~29~30 1997 AT THE FILLMORE

45.1 The Flying Other Brothers, 2006, Chris Shaw

BEHIND THE SCENES IN THE

HIPPIE LOVE CULTS

47.1 Audioslave, 2005, Jeff Wood (Drowning Creek Studio)
48.1 Audioslave, 2005, Jeff Wood (Drowning Creek Studio)

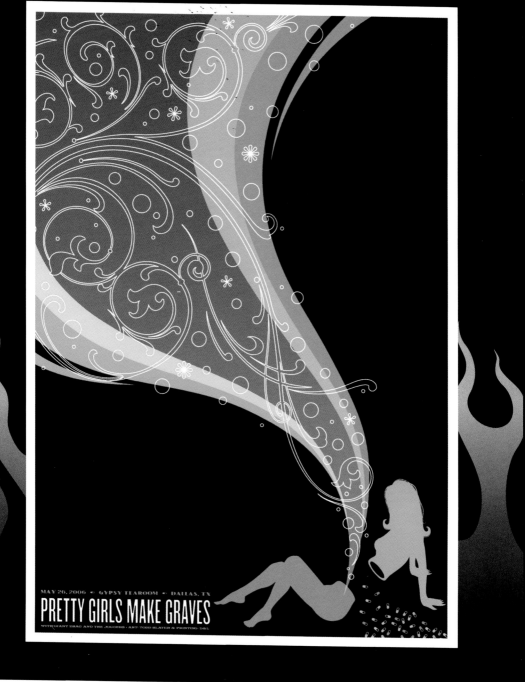

49.1 Pretty Girls Make Graves, 2006, Todd Slater

51.1 David Grisman Quintet, 1997, Jim Phillips (AoMR 291.3)

53.1 Common Sense, 2002, Scrojo (AoMR 467.02)

WILD AND WICKED

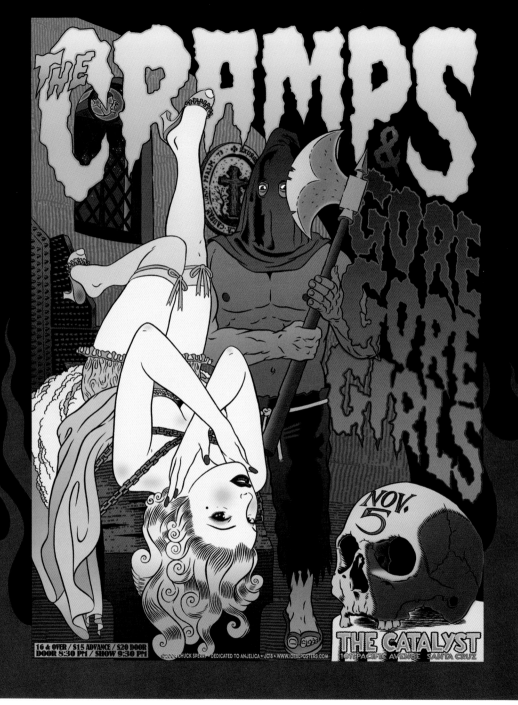

55.1 The Cramps, 2004, Firehouse (Chuck Sperry)

57.1 Dr. Mom, 2003, Elizabeth Daggar (Electrofork)

THE BELLES OF SKIN CITY

MEL GIBSON AND THE PANTS : THE BLIND SHAKE : THE DRAMA CLUB
7TH STREET ENTRY : FRIDAY MARCH 11 : 21+

POSTER BY AMY JO

59.1 Deftones, 2007, Malleus

LIKE, WOW, TOO MUCH

61.1 The Go-Go's, 1994, Su. Suttle

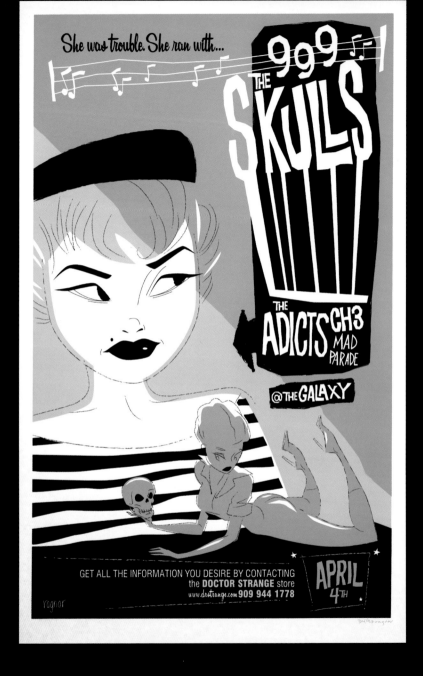

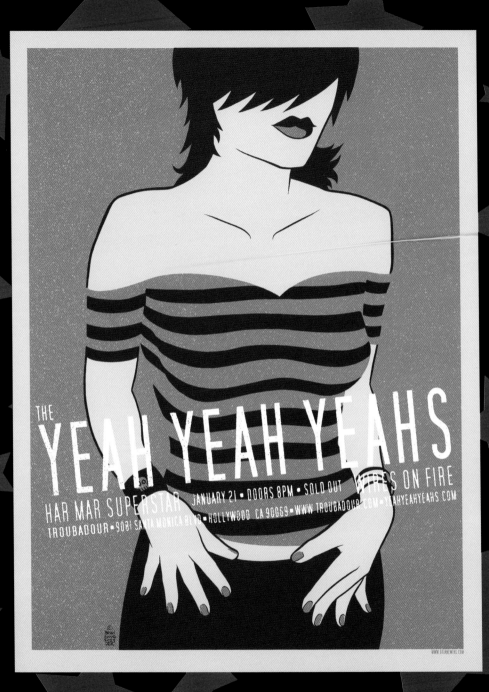

63.1 Yeah Yeah Yeahs, 2004, Brian Ewing
64.1 Psycotic Pineapple, 1994, John Seabury

PRESENTING · IN CONCERT

Loretta LYNN

With THE WRIGHTS
Friday - 2 December 2005
CAIN'S BALLROOM
423 N. Main St., Tulsa, OK
DOORS: 7PM · BOX OFFICE: 918.514.2306
ADVANCE TICKETS: $50 and $42

69.1 Big Sandy and His Fly-Rite Boys, 2005, Scrojo

"Women are powerful in every way.

They rule the world.
I just live in it."

—Stainboy

72.1 Morrisson, 2007, Adam Turman

72 : ART OF MODERN ROCK **POSTER GIRLS**

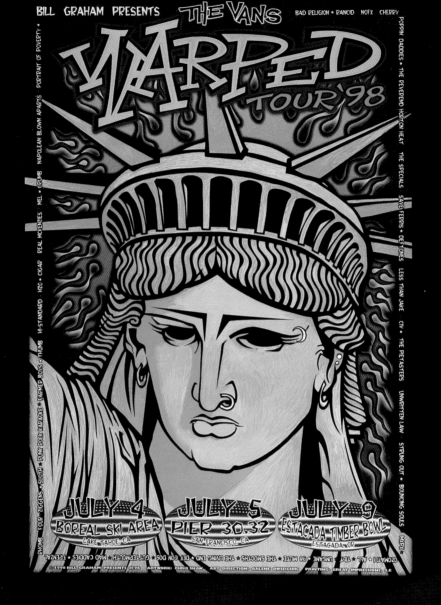

73.1 Vans Warped Tour '98, 1998, Chris Shaw

75.1 Coney Island, 2005, Michael Michael Motorcycle

76.1 Wayne Hancock, 2006, Scrojo

77.1 Reverend Horton Heat, 2003, Scrojo (AoMR 466.12)

IS NUDITY ON POSTERS DEGRADING TO WOMEN?
AN INTERVIEW WITH ART CHANTRY

I've always felt that drawing women is actually a libido exercise for men, even the great artists of the past. The women are always idealized, no matter who they are or how they are drawn. I've always felt that ALL drawings of women by men are fetish art, period.

That being said, I approach design as an assemblage medium. So, I don't feel the need to create my own fetish images to work from; I simply find fetish images that have been forgotten or diminished by time (no longer "sexy" or "dirty" or "obscene" as time goes on) and re-use the anonymous images in new contexts to create new reactions in the viewer. Basically, from a sociopolitical view, I'm usurping the iconography of the "enemy"—in this case, the oppressor who uses stereotyping to demote the power of women.

I want my images to disturb and upset—all the while titillating and appealing to the lizard brain of the male libido. I want the inherent contradiction of that. I want to make the viewer think a little ...

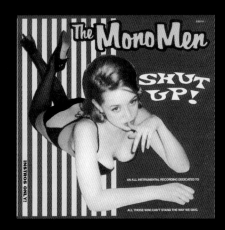

While doing work for Estrus Records, whose Mono Men utilized naked women on their record covers, I discovered a strange thing. At first I dragged my heels on the idea. Being a true-blue Northwest liberal, I found the concept upsetting. I talked at length to the model and the photographer and made sure everybody knew what they were actually doing. They looked at me like I was a fool, and we went ahead with it.

Now, in the early garage-rock scene, many of the power players were women—they ran labels, distributors, stores, bands, 'zines, etc.... Many of the bands were all-women bands, and most of the bands had at least one woman member.

Well, that first nude model we used on a Mono Men cover was a very powerful person. She was well known and is still a major performer in the scene. The response from everyone was a loud cheerful approval. What it did was speak directly to the backward-viewing postmodern culture of garage. The style and the idea and the sheer female empowerment (of female sexuality controlling male responses) of the image inspired most of the women in the scene. All of a sudden we saw dozens of beautiful

Bettie Page wannabes pop up. We saw bands perform old-school striptease. We saw wrestling and cat fights. And strangest of all, we started getting phone calls from these power women demanding to be the next on the Mono Men record cover posing nude.

Subsequently each Mono Men cover began to feature another of these women posing as a delightfully playful "nudie" à la the 1950s men's magazine that your dad used to hide under the mattress. When you represent yourself as a previous generation's sex object, and present yourself in a context where it meant nothing except a contemporary form of banal faddish beauty—it has no more threat. And it becomes your power. However, everybody on the outside of the scene still "hisses" at me, like I'm a pig. I think that's funny. My clients' message strikes home again and again.

79.1 Mono Men, 1992, Art Chantry

EXOTIC
ADVENTURES

81.1 Johnny Winter, 2004, Scrojo
82.1 Queens of the Stone Age, 2003, Emek (AoMR 471.2)

83.1 Jimmy Buffett, 1996, Bob Masse

84.1 The Dresden Dolls, 2006, Malleus

85.1 Hieroglyphics, 2003, Scrojo (AoMR 50.4)

86.1 "Evil Angel," 2001, Firehouse (Ron Donovan)

87.1 Perpetual Groove, 2007, Johnny Thief and Jeff Wood (Drowning Creek Studio)

HAREMS OF PASSION : 87

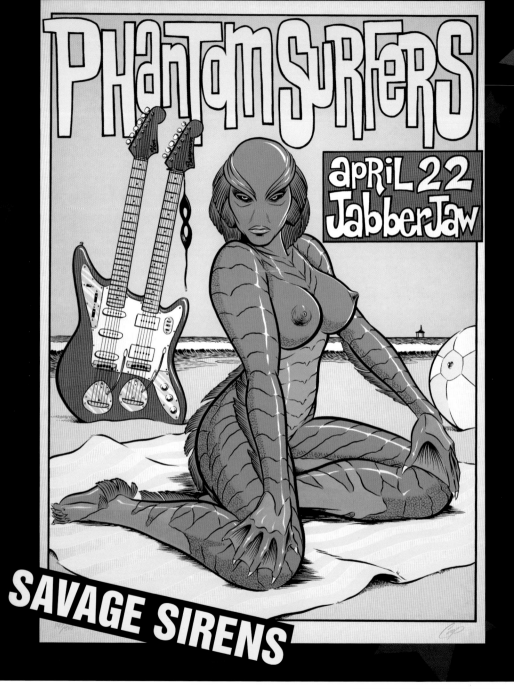

89.1 Dick Dale, 1996, Stainboy

91.1 FMF '07, 2007, Stainboy

SHE'S WILD! SHE'S EXPLOSIVE!

HOUSE OF BLUES ORLANDO · SATURDAY, JANUARY 27
$15.00 ADV / $17.00 DOS · 7:00PM DOORS / 8:00PM SHOW

©2007 HOBO-01 · A STAINBOY VICIOUS IMAGE · WWW.STAINBOYREINEL.COM   PRINTED & FOSSILIZED AT DIESEL FUEL · WWW.DIESELFUELPRINTS.COM

93.1 Mastodon, 2007, Stainboy
94.1 Audioslave, 2003, Firehouse (Ron Donovan) (AoMR 112.1)

64/125

JOMO ETERTAINMENT PRESENTS

JULIANA
HATFIELD
CALEDONIA LOUNGE
ATHENS, GEORGIA
FRIDAY · SEPT 27
TICKETS AT JOMOENTERTAINMENT.COM
POSTER ART BY GOAD AND WOOD
WWW.DROWNINGCREEK.COM · SUPPORT INDIE MUSIC
DCS2-068 ©2002 DROWNING CREEK STUDIO & JASON GOAD

95.1 Juliana Hatfield, 2002, Jason Goad and Jeff Wood (Drowning Creek Studio) (AoMR 486.07)

QUEENS OF THE STONE AGE

with TURBONEGRO

MARCH 15

ATHENS GA
40 WATT CLUB

P.N.E./QOTSA-16

(c) EMEK '03

Trapped by the
fires of hell

BERLIN

03.06.04

www.thecoachhouse.com   phone: 949.496.8930

THE COACH HOUSE
SAN JUAN CAPISTRANO, CA

Poster Design by Will Ruocco   www.willruocco.com

97.1 Queens of the Stone Age, 2003, Emek
98.1 Berlin, 2004, Will Ruocco

99.1 The Cramps, 2003, Print Mafia (AoMR 92.5)

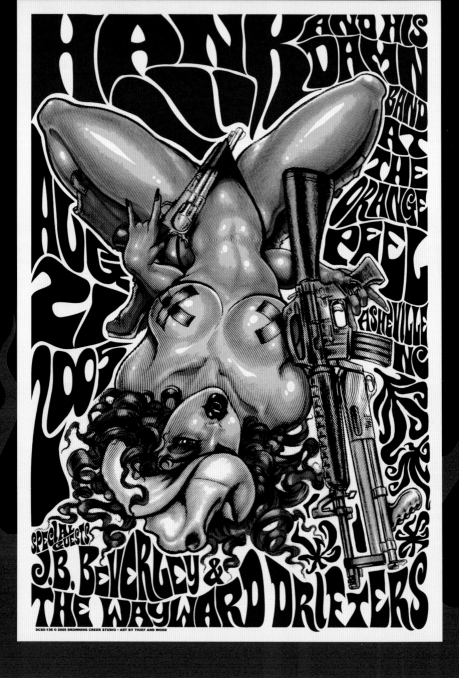

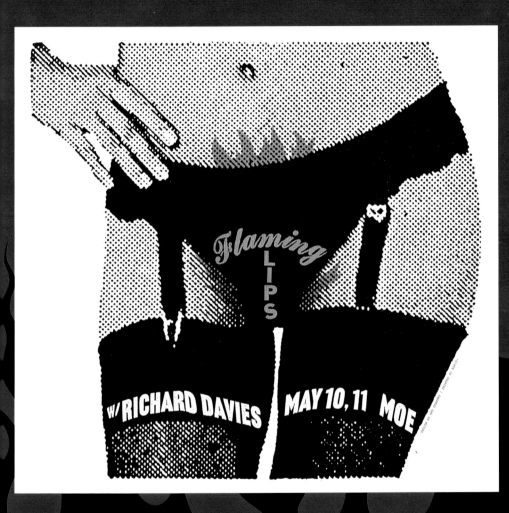

101.1 Flaming Lips, 1995, Art Chantry

102.1 Audioslave, 2005, Jeff Wood (Drowning Creek Studio)

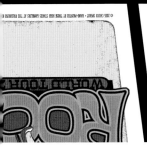

103.1 Art of Modern Rock, 2005, Firehouse (Chuck Sperry)

104.1 Electric Frankenstein, 1998, Coop (AoMR 172.4)

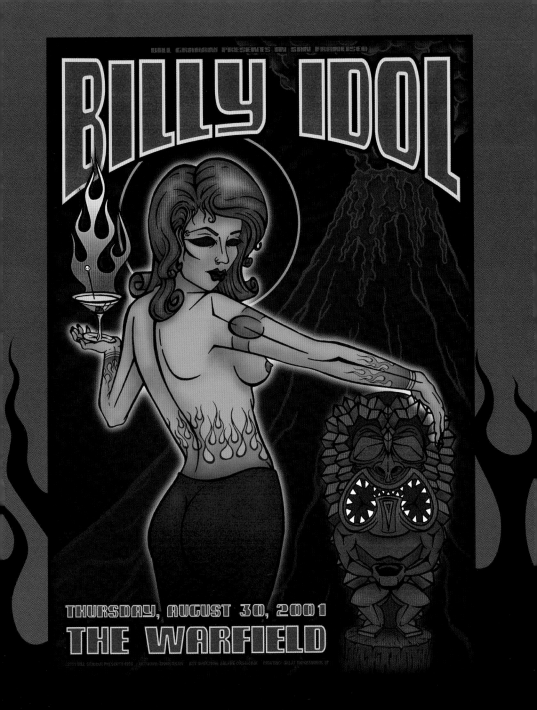

105.1 Billy Idol, 2001, Chris Shaw (AoMR 456.6)

LOVE ON THE PROWL

SATURDAY
MAY 8TH
FIRST AVE.
MAINROOM
$10 ADV
$12 DR
6 P.M. 21+ID

SQUAD19.COM

106.1 Peaches, 2004, Cory Tobin and Steve Tenebrini (Squad 19)

108.1 King Kora, 2001, Michel Casarramona (AoMR 425.3) **108.2** Deerhoof, 2003, Leia Bell (AoMR 448.1) **108.3** Hanin Elias, 2003, Meeloo G'Feller & Anna Hellsgard (Bongout) (AoMR 420.3)

109.1 Bouncing Souls, 2006, Adam Turman

THESE
KITTENS
DON'T PURR

The Bronx • Big Business • Buried Inside • at Bowery Ballroom • NYC • February 3rd 2006

Art by Tara McPherson • Silkscreened by Diesel Fuel Prints • www.dieselfuelprints.com • www.taramcpherson.com

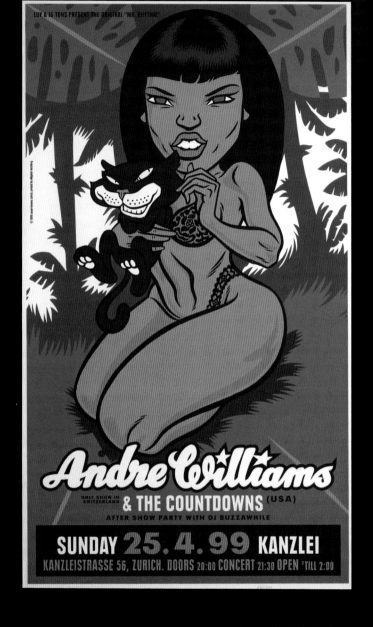

113.1 The Donnas, 2001, Alan Forbes (AoMR 280.2) **113.2** Social Distortion, 2006, Uncle

114.1 The Toasters, 2006, Adam Turman

115.1 Speedball, 1997, Glenn Barr (AoMR 79.4)

THE UNHOLY ALLIANCE TOUR WITH

MASTODON

SLAYER • LAMB OF GOD • CHILDREN OF BODOM • THINE EYES BLEED

JUNE 16TH, 2006 AT THE CONTINENTAL AIRLINES ARENA IN EAST RUTHERFORD, NEW JERSEY

ICE PRINCESS ARTWORK BY TARA MCPHERSON • WWW.TARAMCPHERSON.COM • FROSTY SILKSCREENING BY DIESEL FUEL PRINTS • WWW.DIESELFUELPRINTS.COM

116.1 Mastodon, 2006, Tara McPherson

117.1 L7, 1995, Ellen Forney (AoMR 257.1)

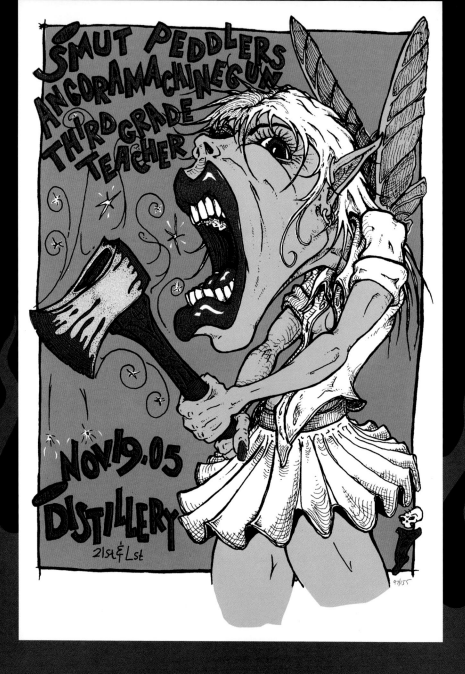

118.1 Smut Peddlers, 2005, Paul Imagine

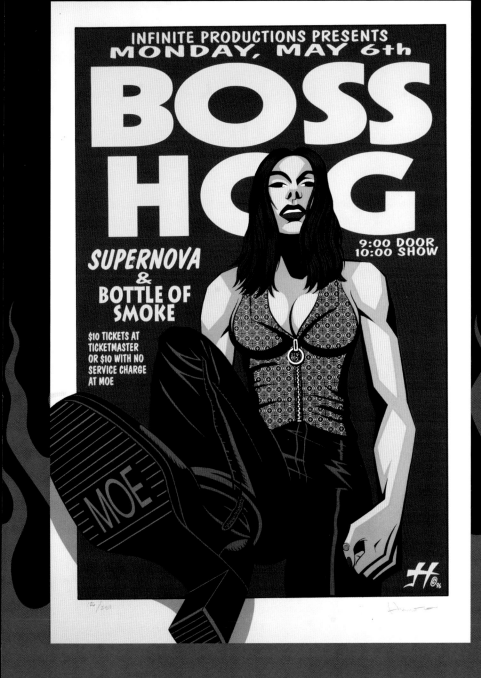

119.1 Boss Hog, 1996, Justin Hampton (AoMR 58.3)

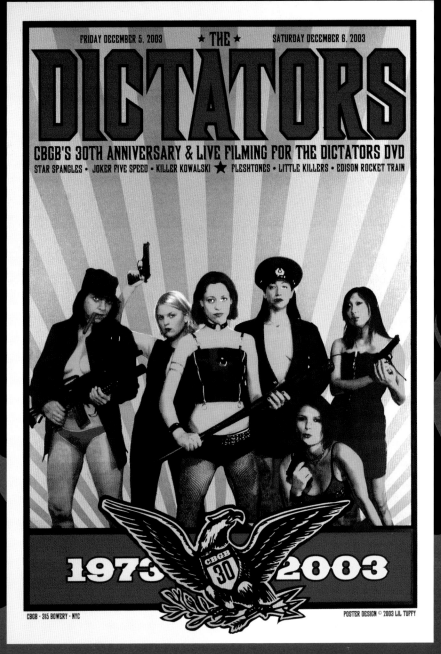

121.1 The Dictators, 2003, L'il Tuffy

WHAT MAKES A
GIRL GO BAD?

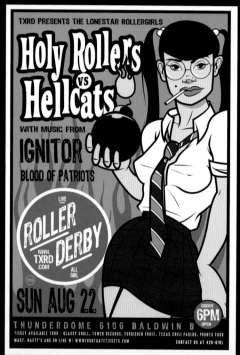

122.1 The Lonestar Rollergirls, 2004, Scrojo **122.2** Chapter Seven, 2003,
Mike Thompson (AoMR 387.5)

123.1 Pretty Girls Make Graves, 2003, Heads of State (AoMR 380.2)

FREE BEFORE **10**

$ **5** $

AFTER

9PM TO 2AM

ENJOY LARGE

DANCE FLOOR

CHEAP DRINKS

& ARCADE

STARTS SATURDAY JULY 31

FEATURING DJs HARLOT CYRUS IVO DEMON LELLY & INTRODUCING DJ HEX

21+

CLIMAX LOUNGE

2217 WELTON ST 1-303-292- LIVE

An understanding study of twisted emotion

GOTHIC • INDUSTRIAL • DEATHROCK • 80'S

DIE BAR **CLUB SUBVERSION**

DENVER, CO

FIRST PRINTING ANYWHERE

124.1 Club Subversion, 2004, R. Black

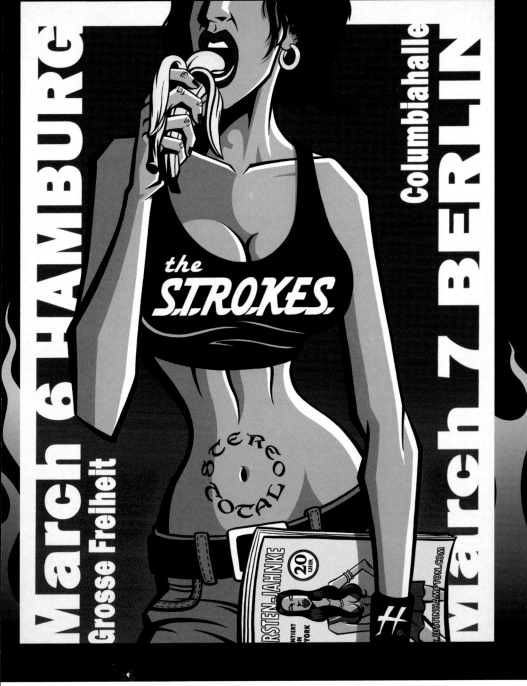

125.1 The Strokes, 2002, Justin Hampton (AoMR 63.2)

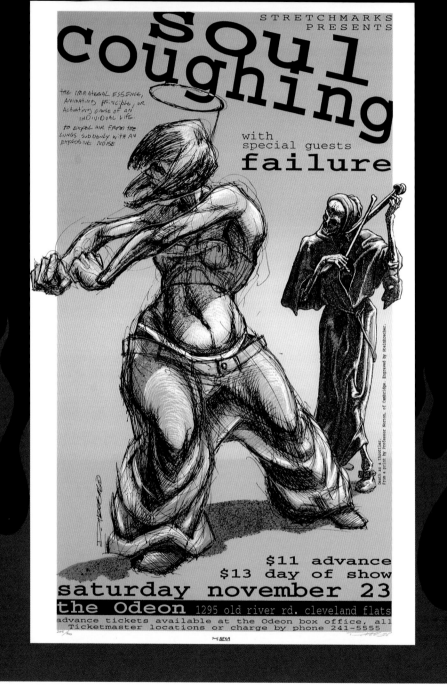

STRETCHMARKS
PRESENTS

soul coughing

with
special guests
failure

the immaterial essence, animating principle, or actuating cause of an individual life.

to expel air from the lungs suddenly with an explosive noise

Death as a throttler. From a print by Professor Morton, of Cambridge. Engraved by Steinbrecher.

$11 advance
$13 day of show
saturday november 23
the Odeon 1295 old river rd. cleveland flats
advance tickets available at the Odeon box office, all
Ticketmaster locations or charge by phone 241-5555

126.1 Soul Coughing, 1996, Derek Hess (AoMR 85.1)

127.1 Arminski Germany—1999, 1999, Mark Arminski (AoMR 82.2)

SEX ON
WHEELS

Super Suckers

PLUS SOME OTHER SHITTY BANDS

SATURDAY
APRIL 19
2003

FULLERTON
TRANSPORTATION
CENTER

©ALMERA

N CONJUNCTION WITH O.C. EARTHDAY   120 E. SANTA FE AVE   FULLERTON, CA

OLOR HANDPULLED IN NEWPORT BEACH, CALIFORNIA

/500

E OF BLUES PRESENT

EADY FOR THE BIG FRIGGIN EVE WITH

ENDUST

AND
GUESTS BURN SEASON
REVELATION THEORY
AM CONSPIRACY

$38 50 ADV. $41 50 DOS - 8PM DOORS / 8:45 PM SHOW

OFFICE AND ALL TICKETMASTER LOCATIONS. FOR MORE
. PRICES, EVENTS, ARTISTS, DATES AND TIMES ARE
CHARGES. NO CAMERAS, VIDEOS OR BACKPACKS ALLOWED.

HEMI-POWERED PRINTING BY DIESEL FUEL • WWW.DIESELFUELPRINTS.CO

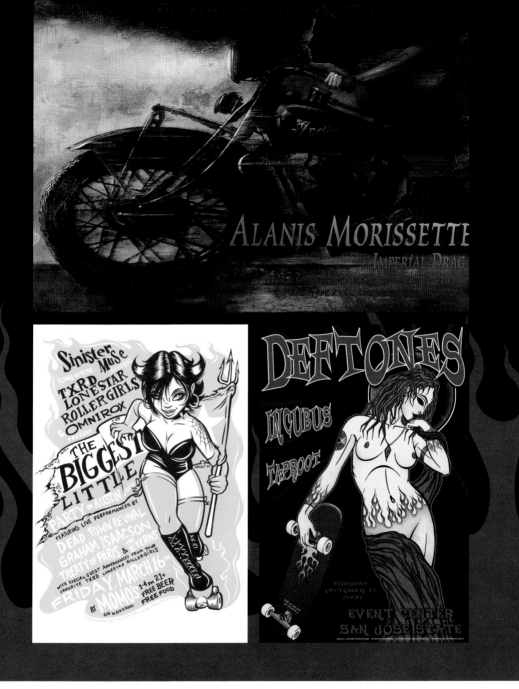

133.1 Alanis Morissette, 1996, Randel Chavez (AoMR 461.1) 133.2 The Biggest Little
Party in Austin 2007, 2007, Adam Turman 133.3 Deftones, 2000, Chris Shaw

134.1 Paul Westerberg, 2005, Scrojo

135.1 The Go-Go's, 2004, R. Black

136.1 Kinky, 2002, Scrojo (AoMR 463.4)

137.1 Bikini Machine, 2006, Tanxxx

138.1 Topless, U.S.A.!, 1993, Frank Kozik (AoMR 31.4)

139.1 The Bastard Sons of Johnny Cash, 2005, Scrojo

WANNA RUB THEM ONCE FOR GOOD LUCK?

The First Annual Meeting of
The POISON 13
Appreciation Society.

with entertainment by

THE LORD HIGH FIXERS
GIRL TROUBLE
BOTTLE OF SMOKE
THE INHALENTS

R.S.V.P.

Attendance
is Advised

5.24.95

MOE

S.C.O.T.S SANCTIONED

Art Chantry

140.1 The Lord High Fixers, 1995, Art Chantry

141.1 Afro Celts, 2003, Scrojo

142.1 The Black Crowes, 2006, Todd Slater

143.1 Ed Hall, 1995, Jason Austin (AoMR 472.5)

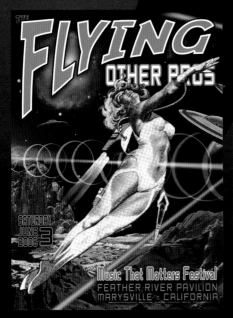

145.1 The Flying Other Brothers, 2006, Chris Shaw **145.2** Sonic Rocket, 2007, Malleus
145.3 Rock Art Expo '94, 1994, Scott McDougall (AoMR 477.1) **145.4** The Nein, 2005, Brian Ewing

146.1 The Spice Girls, 1998, Jason Mecier

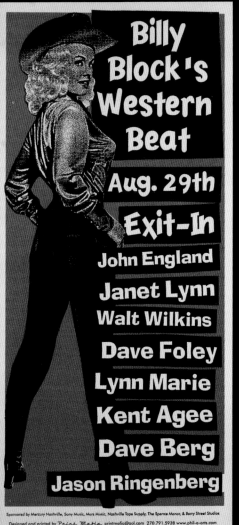

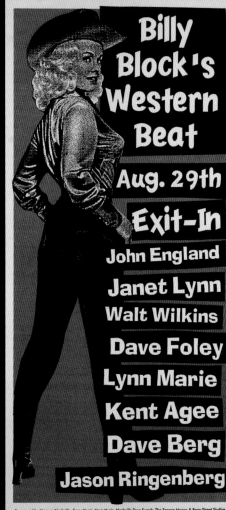

147.1 Billy Block's Western Beat, 2000, Print Mafia (AoMR 177.4)

148.1 Margaret Cho, 1999, Winston Smith

149.1 Dragons, 2002, Firehouse (Chuck Sperry) (AoMR 112.2)

WHY WOLVES WHISTLE

150.1 Joan Jett and the Blackhearts, 2006,
Amy Jo Hendrickson **150.2** Pavement, 1995, John Seabury (AoMR 152.5)

151.1 U2, 2001, Bob Masse (AoMR 210.1)

152.1 Stevie Salas, 2004, Scrojo

153.1 Duran Duran, 2005, Tara McPherson

155.1 British Invasion Night Part Two, 2006, John Seabury

EXPOSED

156.1 The Fall, 2004, Tara McPherson

157.1 Calexico, 2006, Malleus

158.1 Smokewagon, 2003, Elizabeth Daggar (Electrofork)

159.1 PJ Harvey, 2004, Emek

NUDE GODDESSES

26 - 28 NOVEMBRE 2004 IN FAENZA   MEETING ET

© Art by Malleus ᴂ - www.malleusdelic.com - All the names and logos are properties of t

160.1 MEI, 2004, Malleus

TTE INDIPENDENTI 2004

wners

"I'm a fan
of nudity.

In fact,

I'm naked
right now."

—Paul Imagine

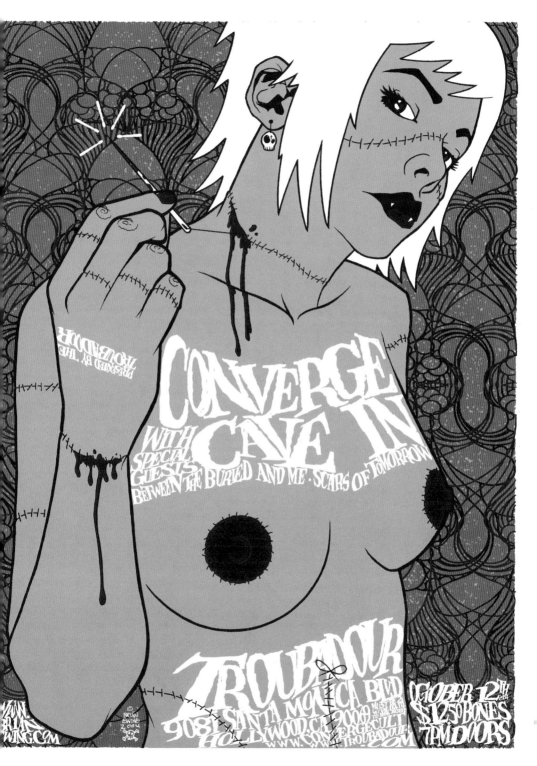

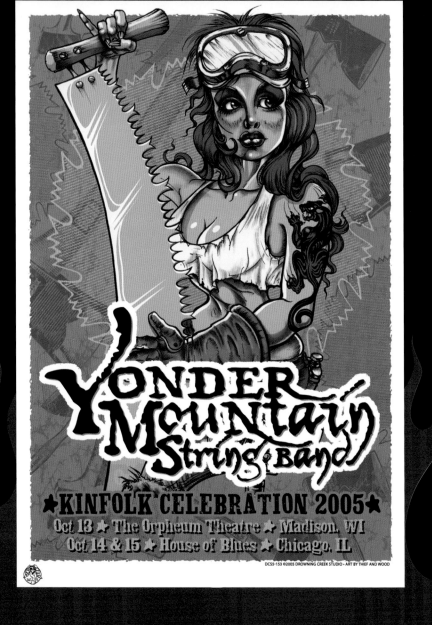

163.1 Converge, 2004, Brian Ewing
164.1 Yonder Mountain String Band, 2005, Johnny Thief and Jeff Wood
(Drowning Creek Studio)

165.1 Yonder Mountain String Band, 2005, Johnny Thief and
Jeff Wood (Drowning Creek Studio) **165.2** The Hopefuls, 2006,
Adam Turman **165.3** Veruca Salt, 2005, Adam Turman

CAUTION: WOMEN AT WORK : **165**

166.1 Optical Hot Dish, 2005, David Witt, Adam Turman, Cory Tobin, and Steve Tenebrini (Squad 19)

168.1 Delta Head, 2007, Malleus

169.1 Devo, 2005, Scrojo

GIRL
POWER

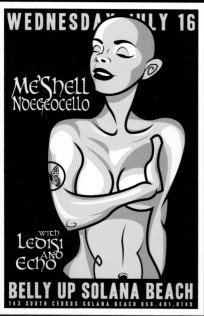

171.1 White Stripes, 2003, Rob Jones
172.1 Tori Amos, 1994, Pamela Hobbs **172.2** Yes, 2002, Scott Benge (FGX)
(AoMR 215.1) **172.3** Me'Shell Ndegeocello, 2003, Scrojo (AoMR 465.2)

173.1 Shonen Knife, 2005, Tara McPherson

174.1 Liz Phair, 1995, Mark Arminski

175.1 Summerfest, 2004, Scrojo

"I think an artist's tendency is to draw what's familiar, and for me that is drawing the female figure. I'm drawn to the softer curves and lines of the female form."

—Tara McPherson

176.1 Green Day, 2005, Tara McPherson

177.1 Fiona Apple, 1998, Bob Masse

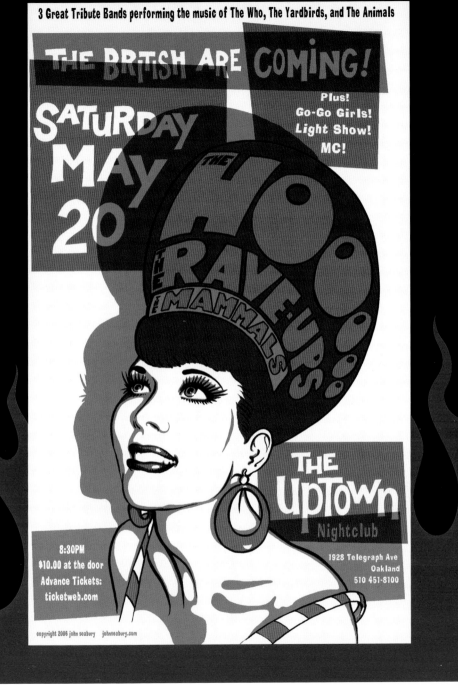

179.1 The Hooooo, 2006, John Seabury

180.1 Isobel Campbell and Mark Lanegan, 2007, Malleus

181.1 Perpetual Groove, 2007, Johnny Thief and Jeff Wood (Drowning Creek Studio)

182.1 Neko Case, 2003, Lindsey Kuhn (AoMR 129.3) **182.2** Mountain, 2002, Dennis Loren **182.3** Patti Smith Band, 2007, Mark Arminski

184.1 Angora Machine Gun, 2006, Paul Imagine

"When does a poster

cross the line?

To get to the other side."
—John Seabury

187.1 Erykah Badu, 2005, Emek

There is nothing more tempting than a scantily clad woman hawking a product.
—R. BLACK

There is a difference between erotica and pornography. I think some of my art lies in the erotic arena because my intention with those pieces is to elicit a sensual response. Sexuality is an essential part of human nature; we are sexual creatures, and I feel it is important to explore that aspect of our existence through art and literature.
—TARA MCPHERSON

On the whole, Scrojo draws my favorite women on posters; they're quirky and individual. Some look devilish and some look like they are holding a secret—they're not just typical iconic sexy women.
—ELIZABETH DAGGAR

I love pinups, especially those from the '30s–'50s. They are sexy and innocent at the same time, which is why they are so appealing.
—KRISTEN THIELE

Women are just more fun to draw. Their features are typically more attractive, their curves, their general shape is very pleasing. But I don't draw women to portray sex, lust, or even feminism. To me, they portray wonder and beauty—an innocence and passion that you can experience while watching your favorite band.
—SARA TURNER (CRICKET PRESS)

It's amazing to me that the nude form, male or female, is still so shocking to so many people. Europe doesn't have the same hang-ups as here in America; they are more steeped in the tradition of arts and culture, and the nude form has always been a part of that.
—JUSTIN HAMPTON

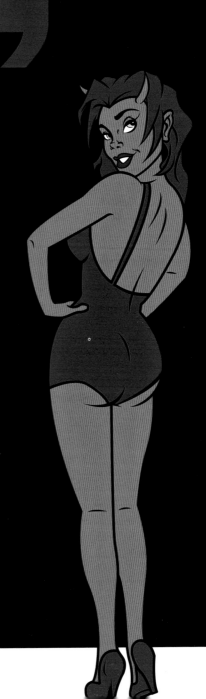

As loath as I am to admit it, under this brutish misogynistic black-hearted thug lives a closet feminist.
—JOHNNY THIEF

I draw really curvy women all the time because they make me happy. I'm grossed out by the media's obsession with anorexic bobbleheads with weird fake boobs so I draw naturally curvy ladies like the ones I know.
—MISTER REUSCH

Is nudity on posters degrading to women? Absolutely not! There's a difference between nudity and nakedness, and that difference is in the context of the poster.
—SARA TURNER (CRICKET PRESS)

My attorney once told me, "Breasts! Guys love 'em, girls love 'em . . . you can't go wrong." It was great advice. Always try to include at least one breast in my artwork.
—CHRIS SHAW